Boys' and Girls' Encyclopedia

Jean Stroud

HAMLYN

London · New York · Sydney · Toronto

The publishers wish to thank the following artists for their contributions:

Norman Barber
Ralph Coventry
Gordon Davies
Ian Garrard
Gwen Green
Harry Green
Brian Lubrani

Richard Orr
John Rignall
George Thompson
Peter Thornley
Carlo Tora
Brian Watson
Walter Wright

The illustrations on page 63 are by courtesy of the General Post Office
and Thames Television

First published 1973
Second Impression 1974
Published by The Hamlyn Publishing Group Limited
London · New York · Sydney · Toronto
© Copyright The Hamlyn Publishing Group Limited 1973

ISBN 0 600 34415 0

Printed by Litografía A. Romero, S. A.
Santa Cruz de Tenerife, Canary Islands (Spain)
D. L. TF. 1.256 - 73

Contents

The Universe 8

How Life Began 10

Prehistoric Animals 12

Mankind 14

Homes 16

The World of Work 20

They Made History 24

Trees 26

Flowers 28

Fruit and Vegetables 30

Mammals 32

Birds 34

Fishes and the Seashore 36

Reptiles and Amphibians 38

Insects 40

Pets 42

The Wonders of Nature 44

The Weather 48

Exploring beneath the Sea 50

Boats and Ships 52

Motor Cars 54

Railways 56

The Story of Flight 58

Man in Space 60

Communications 62

The World of Art 64

Musical Instruments 66

Sports 68

The Universe

The Universe is made up of the Earth we live on, the Sun and its other planets, thousands of other small bodies – and space itself. The Solar System is only a tiny part of the Universe. The Sun is the centre of the Solar System. Nine big planets revolve round the Sun. Our Earth is one of them. The others are Mercury, Venus, Mars, Jupiter, Saturn, Uranus, Neptune and Pluto. A planet is a big ball of rock and gas. The Earth is millions of miles from the sun. The Sun is very important to us. It gives us light and warmth. Some planets, like the Earth, have satellites revolving round them. The Moon is the Earth's satellite. It is closer to the Earth than the Sun. When we see the Sun in the sky it looks large and round and bright. This is because it is the nearest star to us. It is one of millions of stars that make up the Universe. The other stars we see in the sky look small. They are very much further away from us than the Sun. The Sun and all the other stars are very hot. They are made of gases. A galaxy is a mass of stars. If you look at the sky on a dark night you will see a vast number of stars stretching across the sky. They are whirling about in space. These belong to our galaxy, the galaxy of which the Sun is a part. Our galaxy is called the Milky Way. There are millions of galaxies in the Universe. Smaller groups of bright stars are called constellations. Man has been able to use his knowledge of the stars to guide himself during his journeys over the surface of the Earth.

1	Sun	3	Venus	5	Mars	7	Saturn	9	Neptune
2	Mercury	4	Earth	6	Jupiter	8	Uranus	10	Pluto

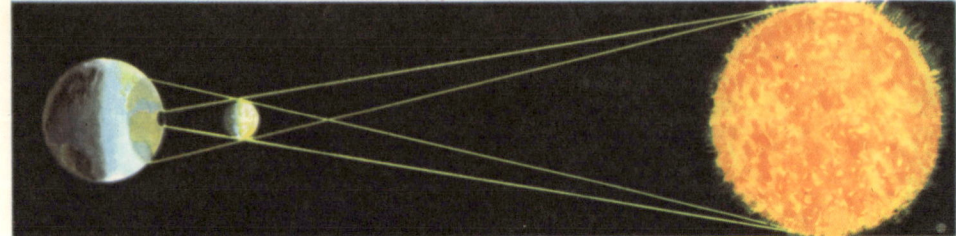

Above: The planets which compose the Solar System. **Left:** An eclipse of the Sun by the Moon. **Below:** The Milky Way galaxy. **Opposite page:** The big radio telescope at Jodrell Bank, Cheshire, England.

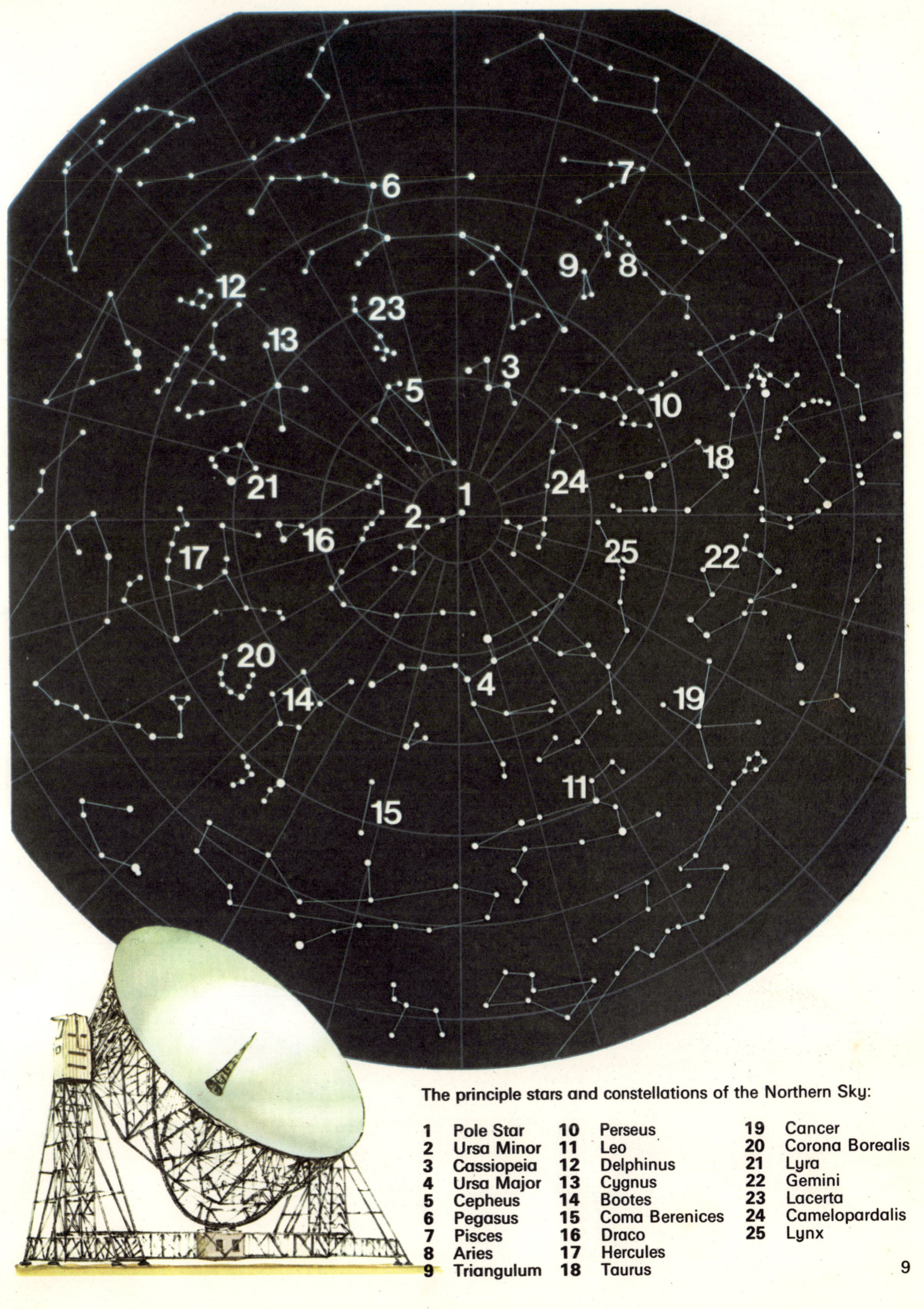

The principle stars and constellations of the Northern Sky:

1	Pole Star	10	Perseus	19	Cancer
2	Ursa Minor	11	Leo	20	Corona Borealis
3	Cassiopeia	12	Delphinus	21	Lyra
4	Ursa Major	13	Cygnus	22	Gemini
5	Cepheus	14	Bootes	23	Lacerta
6	Pegasus	15	Coma Berenices	24	Camelopardalis
7	Pisces	16	Draco	25	Lynx
8	Aries	17	Hercules		
9	Triangulum	18	Taurus		

How Life Began

Millions of different animals and plants live on the earth and in the sea. We know very little about early life. It may have started in some ancient sea many years ago. But we do know that the first forms of life must have been very simple and very small. The first living things were plants. The first plants must have looked like small pieces of green jelly floating in the sea. The first animals must have been small one-celled creatures. The most important thing about them was that they could reproduce. Living things move, feed and breathe. They grow and have young. Conditions are always changing. At

one time seas dried up and became plains. Continents were flooded. Ice covered the land. Mountains, lakes and deserts formed. Forests grew. Animals and plants changed and developed, too. This process of gradual change is called evolution. Animals and plants living now are descended from those which lived long ago. The first animals did not have backbones. Animals without backbones are called Invertebrates. Then Vertebrates – animals with backbones – appeared. Fishes swam in the seas. Life spread to the land.

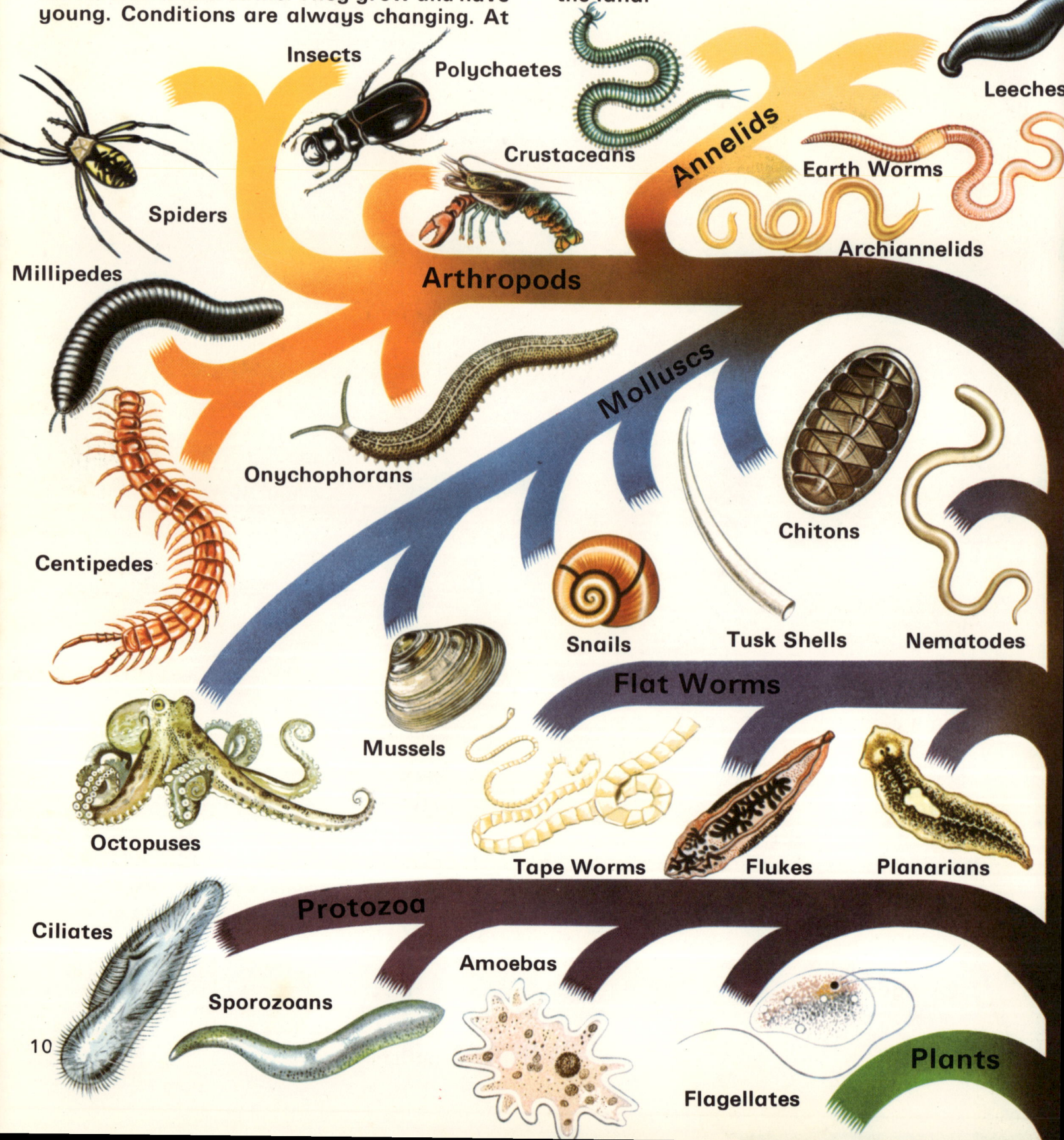

Insects

Polychaetes

Leeches

Spiders

Crustaceans

Annelids

Earth Worms

Millipedes

Arthropods

Archiannelids

Onychophorans

Molluscs

Chitons

Centipedes

Snails

Tusk Shells

Nematodes

Flat Worms

Mussels

Octopuses

Tape Worms

Flukes

Planarians

Protozoa

Ciliates

Sporozoans

Amoebas

Plants

Flagellates

10

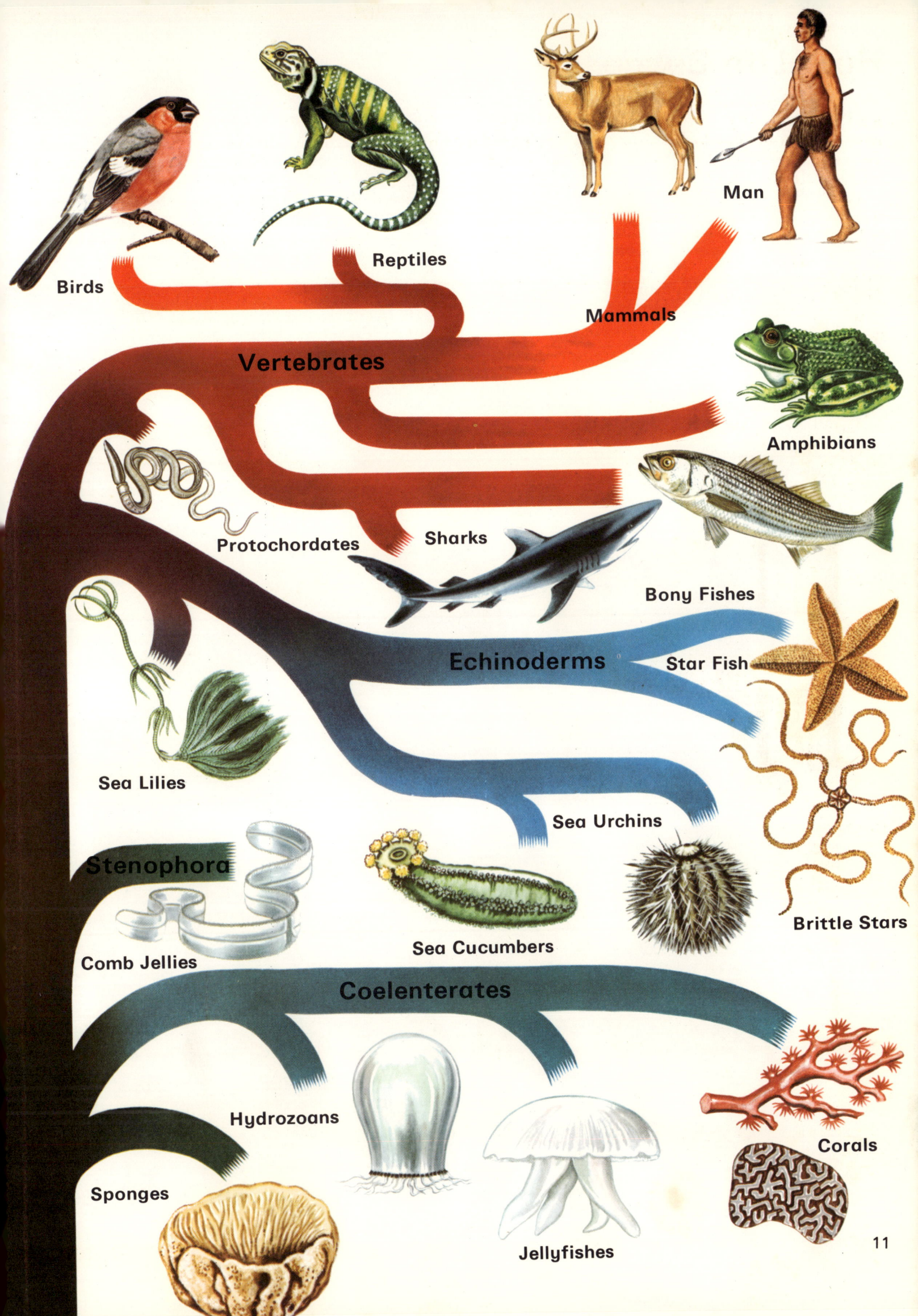

Birds

Reptiles

Mammals

Man

Vertebrates

Amphibians

Protochordates

Sharks

Bony Fishes

Echinoderms

Star Fish

Sea Lilies

Sea Urchins

Stenophora

Sea Cucumbers

Brittle Stars

Comb Jellies

Coelenterates

Hydrozoans

Corals

Sponges

Jellyfishes

Prehistoric Animals

Long before men lived on earth large reptiles roamed the land. They were called dinosaurs. The word dinosaur means 'terrible lizard'. Some dinosaurs were quite small. They were not much bigger than a chicken. Others were gigantic. The biggest known land animal was Brachiosaurus. Brachiosaurus weighed about twenty times as much as a large elephant. He fed on plants. Another great dinosaur was Megalosaurus. He liked to eat meat. He ran on his hind legs, using his tail to balance. Tyrannosaurus was the largest flesh-eating animal that ever roamed the earth. He was one of the last of the dinosaurs. Tyrannosaurus preyed on plant-eating dinosaurs. This big beast had claws on his hind feet. Iguanodon lived on the borders of lakes. In the waters of the lakes lived Brontosaurus. He had a small head, a long neck and a large body with a very long tail. Stegosaurus had bony plates down his back. He had a spiky tail and a very tiny brain. Great sea monsters called Plesiosaurs swam in the sea. The earliest known bird is the Archaeopteryx. It was about the size of a pigeon. It had claws on its wings – and it had teeth. Dinosaurs are extinct. They died out millions of years ago. Mammals took their place. We can tell a lot about these animals from fossils. Fossils are the remains of animals or plants which lived long ago.

Pteranodon, a giant flying reptile, lived in North America.

Above Tyrannosaurus, or 'tyrant lizard', the most famous of all the carnivorous reptiles.

Below Iguanodon had webbed feet, a thick heavy tail, and spikes on his thumbs.

Left Brachiosaurus had a long, heavy neck. He was slow-moving and clumsy on land and stayed in the water most of the time.

The Archaeopteryx, the first true bird. It developed from a reptile.

Ichthyosaurus, a reptile which was completely adapted to life in the sea.

Left The evolution of the modern horse from Eohippus.

a

b

d

c

The fossils shown in this drawing are:
(a) a fern
(b) a crab
(c) a leaf
(d) an ammonite.

Mankind

Human races are sometimes divided into four groups – Negroid, Mongoloid, Caucasoid and Australoid. Some races have black skins, others have white or yellow skins. The shape of the head varies and the texture of the hair differs – it may be dark or fair, straight or curly. The eyes, nose and mouth vary from race to race. Man is the most advanced animal on earth today. Man is different from other animals. He can stand upright. He has a very clever brain. He can think – and reason. He can use his thumb separately from his fingers. Early man soon found he could carry things in his hands. He learned to make and use tools. We know what some of man's early ancestors were like by looking at fossil bones. The first men looked rather like apes. But they walked upright and did not crouch like apes.

Remains of Neanderthal Man were found in Germany, France, Italy and Belgium. Neanderthal Man killed bears and used their skins for clothing. He lived in a cave and used fire for warmth and probably cooking. When Neanderthal Man died out the real ancestor of modern man developed. He is called Cro-Magnon Man. He was a cave-dweller, too, and made beautiful weapons and tools from bone and stone. He hunted

Below Java Man lived about half a million years ago. These Stone Age hunters made weapons and tools from bone and stone.

Neanderthal Man was short, thick-set and powerful. He hunted, made tools, used fire and lived in caves.

Peking Man is known to have used fire.

for food and for clothing. He decorated the walls of his caves with paintings of deer and bison. Then Neolithic, or New Stone Age, Man appeared. The animals, the plants and the climate were much the same on earth then as they are now. Neolithic Man settled in villages and began to trade. This was the beginning of civilization.

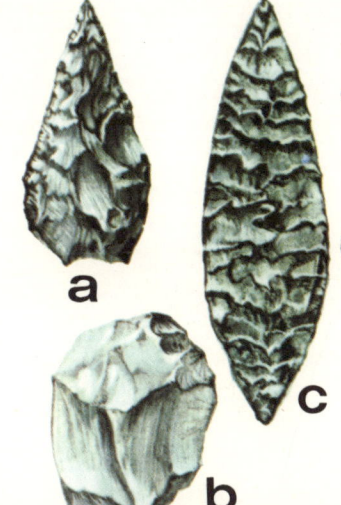

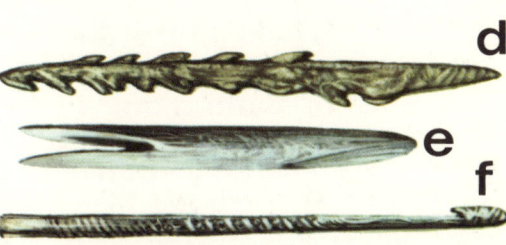

Flint, stone and bone implements
(a) hand axe
(b) quartz chopper
(c) 'laurel leaf' flint
(d) barbed harpoon head
(e) bone lance
(f) spear-thrower

Beautiful cave paintings have been found in many places. Many of the paintings, like these bison, are of the animals hunted by men who lived long ago.

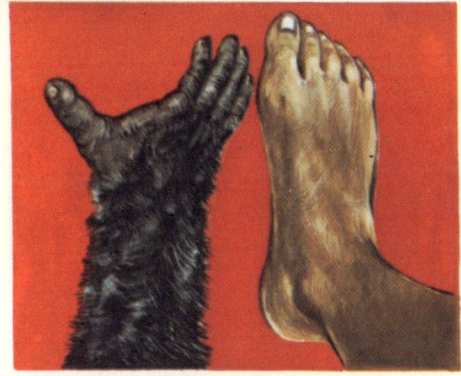

A comparison between an ape foot and a human foot.

The Cro-Magnon race was similar to the people of today. Their homes were designed to last longer than their predecessors'.

Mongoloid

Caucasoid

Negroid

15

Homes

The first men had no homes. They hid in trees or sheltered in caves. Man had to protect himself from wild animals and from his enemies. He needed shelter from the cold and the rain. When man learned to use tools he was able to build many different types of houses. He built huts from branches of trees and made shelters from skins of animals. Ancient Britons lived in 'wattle and daub' huts. Wattle is a kind of basket work. This was smeared all over with wet clay. Egyptians and Babylonians made homes from stone and sun-dried brick. The Greeks covered their walls with a kind of plaster called stucco. The Romans built big villas with brick walls, tiled roofs and mosaic floors. Many small rooms opened off a central courtyard. This courtyard often had a marble basin or pool in the middle. Roman houses had under-floor central heating, kitchens and bathrooms. In warm countries man needs shelter from the sun. In cold countries he needs somewhere he can keep warm. Eskimos made use of the materials available and built their homes of snow-blocks. Arabs wove tents to protect themselves from the sand and sun in the desert.

continued on page 18

Some gipsies still live in caravans as their ancestors did. They are decorated with all sorts of carvings and painted in bright colours — reds, blues, yellows and greens. The caravans used to be drawn by horses but today some are motor-drawn.

In the winter, Eskimos cut blocks of hard snow and fashion them into dome-shaped igloos. The single doorway is entered through a tunnel, and a piece of thin ice forms a skylight.

The Emperor's Palace, Peking. Note the shape of the roof, protecting the palace from the bright sunshine and the monsoon rains.

A modern Norwegian log house. Wood has always been one of the most important building materials used by man. It is easily cut and fashioned.

The people of Dahomey in French West Africa built their houses on stilts above the lagoon to protect themselves from being attacked by either beasts or men.

continued from page 16

Red Indians lived in wigwams. Some people build houses on stilts in lakes. There are stone huts in Turkey, thatched mud-brick adobe houses in Tunisia, reed houses in Vietnam, and mud-walled houses in South Africa. Wooden houses are found in Japan, and log houses in Norway. Flint and brick, as well as stone are used in England. Some Italian houses are made of marble. In Mongolia round houses are made of fur matted into felt. This gives protection from the cold winds. Modern houses are made of many different kinds of material. There are houses built of brick, stone, wood, concrete blocks, steel, tile and glass brick. Some people have no permanent home. Gipsies live in caravans. Bedouins live in tents. Canal people live in narrow boats.

Nomads wander from place to place. They live in the deserts of Central Asia, in Arabia and Mongolia. Mongolians in the Far East live in felt yurts.

The traditional Japanese house is built of timber.

Mountain chalets in Switzerland have flattish roofs on which the snow can lie. This helps to keep the house warm.

Cotswold cottages are built of golden grey stone from nearby quarries. Houses built of local materials fit well into the landscape.

The high, cylindrical towers of Marina City, Chicago, U.S.A. New materials and new methods of building have made it possible to build large blocks of flats.

The World of Work

Most people spend a great deal of time working. There are many varied and interesting jobs. There is a career for every letter of the alphabet from A to Z — from accountancy to zoology. Almost every job you can think of involves working with people. We work in order to earn money to pay for food, houses and clothing for our families. Many women are housewives. They run the home and bring up children. There are jobs where you work with people giving them a service of some kind such as the postman, milkman, dress-maker, hairdresser. There are office jobs where one deals mainly with books, papers, figures or office machines. There are many jobs for people who are clever working with their hands. Watchmakers, motor mechanics, bricklayers, plumbers and plasterers are craftsmen. There are the practical or technical jobs, making or repairing things. Some people follow what we call the professions, such as doctors, dentists, clergymen, lawyers, teachers. Almost everybody works

continued on page 22

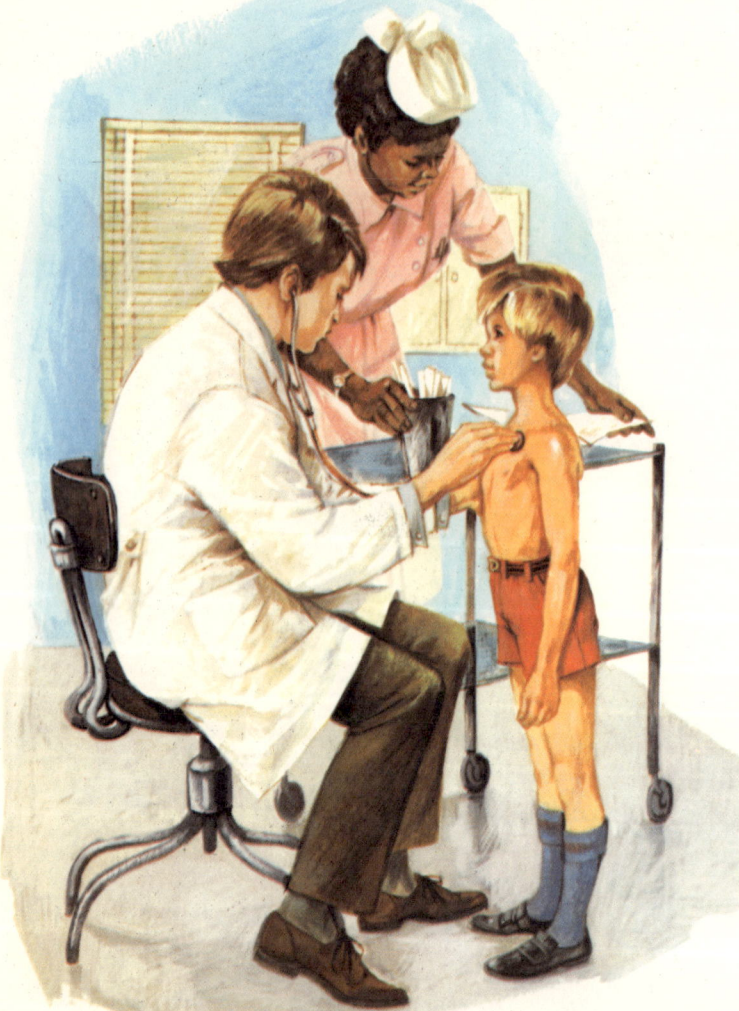

When you feel ill your mother takes you to the doctor. The doctor listens to your breathing with his stethoscope. A nurse helps the doctor. She helps care for sick people.

There is such a lot to learn about everything in the world. Most children attend some kind of school. At school, teachers help children to learn. School teaches children how to use their minds. Grown-ups go to school, too. Even adults do not know all there is to know.

A farmer ploughs furrows in the fields. This breaks up the soil before the seed is sown. He is driving a tractor. In some countries oxen are used to pull ploughs.

Below This bricklayer is building a house. Do you see that the wall is really two walls? This acts as insulation and keeps the house cool in summer and warm in winter.

Above A mechanic repairs a car. He knows the many different parts, where to find them, and the work they do in making the car run smoothly.

The coal miner digs out the hard black rock from the coalface underground. He is wearing a helmet and a lamp. Props hold up the roof after the coal is dug out.

continued from page 20

today. You may not find it easy to decide upon the kind of job you would most like to do. Different jobs need different sorts of people. People differ from one another. They have different skills, abilities and interests. The ideal job is one in which you are paid for doing something that you would enjoy doing anyway. You may need special training to fit you for the job you choose to do. If you like people, are enthusiastic and have an orderly mind, perhaps being a shop assistant will be just the occupation for you. Being a policeman is a very important job. Some people work indoors. Others, like the farmer, work outdoors. To get on with all kinds of people it is essential to be patient and have a sense of humour.

Working with animals can be very interesting and rewarding. Trained dogs work with policemen. They track criminals. Alsatians, Labrador retrievers and Dobermann pinschers are very good at doing this.

'Barber' means one who shaves or trims a beard. The present-day hairdressing salons or barber's shops are very different from earlier shops. At one time barbers were also surgeons. They practised surgery, blood-letting and dentistry. A barber's pole, with red and white spiral stripes hung outside every barber-surgeon's shop.

A shop assistant weighs goods for a customer. Shops used to specialize in a particular line of goods . . . grocers sold groceries, bread was bought from the baker, a draper dealt in textiles and cloth goods. Now large supermarkets and self-service stores sell a wide variety of articles.

A secretary works in an office. She is employed by a person or firm to deal with correspondence, collect information and prepare business papers. A secretary must be able to type and write shorthand. A good telephone manner and a pleasing appearance are important.

Firemen unrolling a hose from a fire-engine. Water pumped through the hose will extinguish the fire.

A baker makes bread and cakes. Bread is baked in a hot oven.

Postmen deliver mail. Air mail and parcel post are unloaded from an aeroplane.

They Made History

From earliest times man has wanted to know more about the world around him. Early explorers sailed out to sea and discovered new lands. They crossed the frozen Arctic wastes. Man climbed mountains, and learned how to fly. He journeyed through space and landed on the moon. Now he is exploring the bottom of the sea. Explorers visited new places and learned new things. Marco Polo made his way by land and sea from Italy to China. Vasco da Gama was the first to reach India by sea from Europe. Christopher Columbus crossed the Atlantic and discovered the New World. Magellan sailed into a great ocean and named it the Pacific. Sir Francis Drake was the first Englishman to sail round the world. Captain Cook explored the coasts of New Zealand and Australia. Speke found the source of the Nile and Stanley explored the Congo. Peary was the first man to reach the North Pole. Scott arrived at the South Pole only to find that Amundsen had reached it before him. Besides exploring, men have also invented things which help people in their everyday lives. Faraday discovered how to make electricity. Without electricity we would not have electric light, telephones, radio or television. Bell invented the telephone. An Italian, Marconi, sent the first signals by wireless. Baird was the first to send pictures by radio. We call his invention television.

Below Dr Alfred Nobel, Swedish chemist and inventor of dynamite. The annual Nobel Prize is named after him.

Above Louis Pasteur, the great French chemist. He discovered that infectious diseases are caused by germs.

Above Robert E. Peary, an American admiral, explored the Arctic. He reached the North Pole on 6 April 1909.

Left Alexander Fleming, a Scottish bacteriologist. He discovered penicillin, which kills or prevents the growth of bacteria harmful to man.

Below William Caxton, the first English printer.

Albert Einstein, German-born mathematical physicist and a great man of science. He is famous for his theories of relativity.

Right Scotsman, Alexander Graham Bell. In 1876 he spoke to his assistant in another room. An electric current carried his words, 'Mr Watson, come here, I want you,' along the wire.

Leonardo da Vinci, celebrated Italian artist, born near Florence. He painted the 'Mona Lisa' and the 'Last Supper'.

Below Captain James Cook, famous English explorer and navigator. He was killed on the shores of Kealakekua Bay, Hawaii in 1779.

Above Galileo Galilei, Italian astronomer, physicist and mathematician. He proved that unequal weights drop with equal velocity. He made his experiment from the leaning tower of Pisa.

Above Sir Isaac Newton, one of the greatest scientists of all time, used a prism to analyze white light; he invented the reflecting telescope and worked out the theory of gravitation.

Ferdinand Magellan, Portuguese seaman and navigator. He sailed down the east coast of South America and was the first European to navigate the straits named after him.

25

Trees

Trees are plants. They have thick woody trunks. Branches spread out from the trunk. From these branches sprout twigs and shoots. The trunk and branches are covered with a layer of bark. There are two main types of tree. One sheds nearly all its leaves in the autumn. This type is called deciduous. The other stays green all the year round. These are called conifers. Conifers, or evergreens, have long, narrow leaves called 'needles'. New needles grow behind the old ones. When the old ones drop off the new ones take their place. Pines are conifers, as are cedars, cypresses, larch and spruce. The most important deciduous tree in Britain is the oak. In olden days, wooden ships were built of the hard, tough timber. The fruit of the oak is the acorn. Other trees which have broad flat leaves like the oak are the ash, beech, birch, elm, hazel, and horse chestnut. The shiny seeds of the horse chestnut are called 'conkers'. Trees get their food from the air and the soil. The leaves take in the air and the sunlight. The roots, which go deep into the ground, absorb water and mineral salts. Trees can live to a very great age. If you look at a sawn off tree trunk you will notice a number of rings. Each ring is one year's growth. Trees supply us with timber. Paper, furniture and tools are made from wood. Oil comes from the fruit of the coconut palm. Rubber is made from the sap of a tree which grows in the East Indies. Maple syrup and maple sugar come from the sap of the sugar maple. Trees are extremely useful plants.

Right The Chile Pine, or Monkey-Puzzle — a native of southern Chile.

Above Mangrove trees grow in tropical swamps.

Right The Traveller's Tree of Madagascar provides water for thirsty passers-by. The sheaths of the leaf stalks contain a refreshing water-like liquid, obtained by cutting the stem.

The Cedar of Lebanon, mentioned many times in the Bible.

The light and graceful Ash tree.

26

The Redwood tree.

The Oak, the largest and longest-lived English tree. Oaks are not usually felled under the age of 200 years.

Above The Lombardy Poplar, introduced into England from Italy.

The hardy Sycamore tree.

The pink or white flowers of the Horse Chestnut are often called 'giants' nosegays'.

The Holly. The leaves are prickly and the berries scarlet and glossy.

27

Flowers

Every flower has a root, stem, leaves, flower and seeds. Each flower has its own shape and colour. Many flowers have one bloom growing on a single stalk. The scarlet poppy and the tulip are large flowers, with brightly-coloured petals. The daisy and dandelion are made up of tiny flowers called 'florets'. The petals of the bluebell and the harebell are joined to form a bell-shaped flower. Flowers produce fruit and seeds from which new plants grow. A flower has many parts. Each part has a special job to do. The petals attract insects with their bright colour and scent. Nectar is stored in sepals at the base of the petals. Bees visit the flowers to collect the nectar from which they make honey. Stamens have big heads called anthers. Anthers contain a very fine powder called pollen. This pollen rubs off on the insects and

they carry it from one flower to another. Sometimes it is blown by the wind. The pollen rubs off on the stigma of a flower and travels inside the long thin style down to the ovary. The seeds start growing there. The carpel covers the seeds and protects them. These seeds may grow into new plants. A plant grows new leaves in the spring; it flowers in the summer and produces fruit and seeds in the autumn. The waterlily is anchored to the bottom of the stream or pond by its roots. The flowers come up on a long stem and open out above the water. Flowers grow in the desert and the jungle. Some plants eat insects. Most trees have flowers. Apple blossom is the flower of the apple tree. The largest flower family in the world is the Daisy Family.

6

7

8

9

10

11

12

13

14

15

1 Orchid
2 Holly
3 Yucca
4 Waterlily
5 Camelia
6 Magnolia
7 Poppy
8 Honeysuckle
9 Dutchman's-breeches
10 Cuckoo pint
11 Crocus
12 Venus fly trap
13 Foxglove
14 Cactus
15 Rose

Fruit and Vegetables

Fresh fruit contains vitamins. We need plenty of vitamins if we are to keep healthy. Every plant has its own kind of fruit. Some fruits such as apples, melons, pears, grapefruit, oranges, figs and pomegranates, have many seeds. Sometimes there is only a single seed such as the stone in a plum, cherry, peach, apricot, walnut, almond and avocado pear. Apricots belong to the plum and peach family. They grow in warm, sunny climates. Bananas grow in tropical climates. They grow on tall plants with huge leaves. Bananas grow in big bunches, which are split into smaller bunches called 'hands' before being sent to the shops. 'Hands' have between ten and fifteen 'fingers'. Figs and dates grow on palm trees in deserts. Citrus fruits – oranges, grapefruit, lemons and limes – grow in warm climates, especially Spain, South Africa, California and Florida. Orange trees are grown from pips. Pawpaws and mangoes are also tropical fruit. Grapes can be eaten as fruit or made into wine. Some grapes are dried in the sun to make raisins, sultanas and currants. The tomato is sometimes called the 'love apple'. Like the gooseberry it has seeds in a juicy pulp enclosed in a skin. Melons and watermelons are large fleshy fruits. The seeds of peas and broad beans grow in pods. We eat the bulb of the garlic and onion and the flower of the cauliflower. We eat the leaves of spinach, lettuce, Brussels sprouts and cabbage. Among the root vegetables we eat are carrots, radishes, parsnips and beetroots. Celery, leeks and rhubarb are plant stems.

Apple

Bananas

Orange

Cherries

Avocado pear

Grapefruit

Strawberries

Pineapple

Grapes

Coconut

Lemon

Pear

Mango

Potatoes

Cauliflower

Turnip

Below Rice paddy field

Peas

Artichoke

Right Purple-sprouting broccoli

Cabbage

Parsnip

Yams

Brussels sprouts

Onion

Carrot

31

Mammals

Mammals are warm-blooded animals. They breathe through lungs. People are mammals. So are dogs and cats, donkeys and horses, cows and pigs, rabbits and monkeys. All mammals have backbones, and nearly all have some hair on their bodies. They feed their young on milk. Some mammals lay eggs. The duck-billed platypus and the spiny anteater of Australia lay soft-shelled eggs. Animals with pouches are called marsupials. Opossums, wombats, kangaroos and koala bears are marsupials. All members of the cat family are meat-eaters or carnivores. African lions are cats, so are cheetahs, jaguars, leopards, the tigers of Asia – and the domestic cat we look after in our homes. The coyote of North America, the dingo of Australia, the hyena of Africa and Asia, wolves and jackals, belong to the dog family.

They are all hunters and feed on meat. Polar bears live in the Arctic. They hunt seals and fish. Polar bears hibernate. They store up food in their bodies during the summer and sleep during the winter. Hedgehogs, dormice and bats also hibernate. Rhinoceroses, moose, antelopes, buffaloes, deer and hippopotamuses are hoofed animals. They have horny pads covering the tips of their toes. Beavers, rats, mice, squirrels, hamsters and chipmunks are rodents. Rodents are plant-eaters. Beavers can gnaw down trees with their sharp teeth. The blue whale is the largest mammal in the world. The world's largest land mammal is the African elephant. The Ape family is most like the family of Man.

Reindeer

Camel

Kangaroo

Panda

Bear

32

Rhinoceros

Elephant

Giraffe

Lion

Chimpanzee

Leopard

Zebra

Tiger

Cheetah

Birds

All birds have feathers. Birds are hatched from eggs. The largest bird in the world is the ostrich. Ostriches are unable to fly. But they have strong legs, and can run very quickly. Penguins cannot fly, but they are strong swimmers. Emperor penguins live in the ice and snow of the Antarctic. Ducks, geese and swans have webbed feet. They are powerful swimmers, and can fly too. Garden birds have feet that can easily grip the branch of a tree. Insect-eating birds have thin pointed beaks. Seed-eaters have short, stubby beaks. Owls are birds of prey. They have strong talons and hooked beaks. Most owls hunt for food by night. Eagles, hawks, falcons and buzzards are also birds of prey. They feed by day. They eat mice and snakes. Birds are warm-blooded. Their body temperature is higher than that of a human.

They fluff themselves out in cold weather to trap the warm air inside. They sing to attract other birds and to guard an area or territory. Some birds such as the mynah and the Mexican yellow-headed parrot can be taught to talk. Not all birds build nests. Some birds lay their eggs among the pebbles on a beach, or in the sand. Cuckoos lay their eggs in other birds' nests. The tiniest birds in the world are the humming birds. Some are no bigger than a bumble bee. They dart about or hover, moving their wings so rapidly that you can hardly see them. They sip nectar from flowers with their slender, curved beaks. Many birds migrate. They fly to warmer climates in the autumn. They fly long distances over land and sea. When spring comes they fly back again, very often returning to the same nesting site.

1   Flesh tearing bill and foot of Peregrine Falcon
2   Nut cracking bill and gripping toes of Macaw
3   Mud probing bill and wading foot of Curlew
4   Nut cracking bill and perching foot of Hawfinch
5   Water filtering bill and swimming foot of Mallard
6   Wood hewing bill and climbing foot of Green Woodpecker
7   Cup-type nest of Chaffinch
8   Leaf cradle stitched by Tailorbird
9   Weaverbird's enclosed nest with funnel entrance
10 Domed nest of Long-tailed Tit

1 Arctic Tern
2 Blue Bird of Paradise
3 Cuckoo
4 Frigate Bird
5 Robin
6 Streamertail Hummingbird
7 Bee Hummingbird
8 Sappho Comet Hummingbird
9 Red Plumed Bird of Paradise
10 Golden Eagle
11 Peacock
12 Tawny Owl
13 Ostrich
14 Lyre Bird

Fishes and the Seashore

Fishes are cold-blooded. They breathe through gills which take air from the water. Fishes can hear, although they have no outer ears or eardrums. They have scales, and fins with which to balance themselves and change direction. Some fish have teeth – they eat other animals. Other fish eat plants and small insects. Freshwater fishes include sticklebacks, minnows, perch, pike, chub, carp, gudgeon, roach, tench and bass. Salmon and trout live in fresh and salt water. They are born in fresh water and swim to the sea for food. Eels are born in the sea but the young eels, or elvers, swim back to the rivers. Most fish lay eggs, but a few have live young. The male catfish carries eggs in its mouth. When they hatch the baby fish use his mouth as a nest. Flying fish do not flap their wings – they glide. Sea-horses swim standing up. They can grip hold of an object with their tails. Halibut and plaice are flat fishes. They live on the sea bed. The largest fish in the sea is the whale shark which lives in warm waters. It is quite harmless. It feeds on the tiny plants and animals called plankton that float on the surface of the oceans. The Portuguese man-of-war is a jellyfish. Jellyfish have hollow bodies and long tentacles. They sting. Sea anemones and corals, starfish, sea-urchins, whelks and squids are some of the many animals that can be found in rocky pools left at low tide or stranded on the sands near the low tide mark.

Below The salmon lays its eggs in fresh water, but feeds, develops and grows in the sea. Salmon often leap clear of the water.

Right Sea anemones are carnivorous animals, not plants. They trap small animals in their tentacles which contain stinging cells. The tentacles resemble flower-like petals.

Below The starfish has five pointed arms extending from the body. The mouth is beneath the body and there is a small red 'eye' at the tip of each arm.

Above Swordfishes are the largest of all true fishes. They weigh anything up to a ton.

Left The Portuguese man-o'-war is unable to swim. It floats freely in the water. The hanging tentacles grow to 60 feet in length. Its sting can be very painful.

Left The whale shark is the largest known fish. It is harmless. It feeds on the small sea animals and plants known as plankton which float on the surface of the seas. Sharks have rounded bodies. They can swim very quickly. The mouth is on the underside of the head.

Above The Halibut is the largest of all the world's flatfishes. The skin is very smooth and of a dark yellowish-green colour.

Below The whisker-like barbels round the mouth have given the Catfish its name. One of the European Catfishes, the Wels, grows to a length of about 10 feet.

Left Eels look rather like snakes. They are long and thin and their smooth, shiny bodies are flattened at the tail.

37

Reptiles and Amphibians

Long ago, before there were any birds or mammals, huge reptiles lived on the earth. The reptiles which live on earth today are descended from these prehistoric monsters. Most reptiles live on land. Reptiles are cold-blooded. This means that their blood takes on the temperature of the air around them. They have dry skins, covered with scales. Crocodiles are the largest members of the reptile family. Alligators are smaller than crocodiles. Most reptiles eat other animals. Tortoises and turtles have shells on their backs and a protective plate on the underside. They can tuck their head and legs inside their shell. Some turtles live in fresh water. Marine turtles live in the sea. The largest lizard is the Komodo dragon. He is covered in black, beady scales and his skin hangs in folds. Lizards have short legs. The Tuatara, a lizard-like reptile, is found only in New Zealand. Snakes are covered with dry scales. They move by pressing their scales against the earth and then wriggling along in a series of 'S' shapes by moving their ribs. The flying-snakes of India live in trees. They can stiffen their bodies and glide from tree to tree. Some snakes are poisonous. The cobra, mamba, viper and rattlesnake all have special teeth called fangs. Amphibians live on land or in water. They have moist, soft skins. The young are called tadpoles. Frogs and toads do not have tails. Salamanders, newts and mud-puppies have tails.

Alligator

Frog

Indian Viper

Tortoise

Salamander

Komodo Dragon

Newt

Toad

Chameleon

Rattlesnake

Crocodile

Python

Boa

Turtle

Anaconda

Insects

Insects are small animals. Grasshoppers, dragonflies, moths, butterflies, wasps, bees, beetles, flies and ants are insects. Insects have six legs, one pair of feelers and usually one or two pairs of wings. The body is divided into three – head, thorax and abdomen. Insects breathe through holes in their skin which lead into air tubes. Ants, bees and wasps live together in families. They are what are called 'social' insects. Some insects are harmful to man – others help him. Insects carry pollen from one flower to another. Ladybirds and lacewings eat other harmful insects. Houseflies spread germs. Mosquitos carry diseases. Female mosquitos suck blood. Horseflies bite. Wasps sting. Fleas and lice live on man and other animals. Small, white creatures called termites eat their way through wood. Dragonflies, mayflies and caddis flies mate while flying. The young are called nymphs. The butterfly has compound eyes – each of its two big eyes is made up of thousands of very small ones. Butterflies lay their eggs on plants. Caterpillars emerge from the eggs. As the caterpillars grow they shed their skins several times. They turn into chrysalises. The skin of the chrysalis bursts and a new butterfly struggles out. Male crickets 'sing' by rubbing their front wings together or by rubbing their front wings with their hind feet. Water scorpions and water boatmen live on and in water. Many insects such as beetles and cockroaches have a hard, thick pair of wings which cover a second folded pair of soft flying wings. Glow-worms are soft-bodied beetles.

1   Swallowtail Butterfly
2   Chalkhill Blue
3   Blue Mountain Swallowtail
4   Lime Hawk Moth
5   Six-Spot Burnett
6   Indian Leaf Butterfly
7   Borneo Birdwing
8   Moon Moth
9   Praying Mantis
10 White-tailed Bumblebee

11 Wasp
12 Beetle
13 Cicada
14 Locust
15 Buprestid Beetle
16 Leaf Insect
17 Dragonfly
18 Stick Insect
19 Grasshopper
20 Stag Beetle
21 Ant

Pets

The earliest pets kept by man were probably hawks. Hawks are hunters and man trained these birds of prey to catch wildfowl and other animals. Dogs have helped man to hunt food from very early times. Spaniels are sporting dogs. Dogs are faithful and intelligent by nature. They make good companions and good pets. Cats like to come and go as they please but they, too, are affectionate animals. Ancient Egyptians regarded them as sacred animals. There are two main types of cat – the long-haired and the short-haired. The Blue Persian is long-haired. The British tortoise-shell and tabby are short-haired, as are the Siamese, Burmese and Abyssinian. Hamsters make wonderful pets. They take up very little space and are cheap to feed. They like to sleep during the daytime. They store food in pouches in their cheeks. Netherland Dwarfs, Flemish Giants, Old English, Chinchilla, Dutch, Himalayan, Lop and Angora are all varieties of rabbits. Rabbits can become very tame. A rabbit should never be picked up by the ears. Guinea pigs were kept as pets by the Incas in Peru many years ago. They are easy to handle and do not bite. Budgerigars originally came from Australia. They are pretty birds and like playthings – mirrors, ladders and balls – in their cage or outdoor aviary. Budgies can be taught to talk. Male canaries sometimes sing. Goldfish are cold water fish. They look attractive in a tank. Gerbils come from the hot, dry, African and Asian deserts. They eat fruit, vegetables and seeds. Pets like company. They like to be talked to, and some like to be handled. They need food and water regularly.

Above Rabbits like two good meals a day. They eat hay and oats, root vegetables such as swedes and carrots, and green vegetables – grass, lettuce, nettles and dandelions.

Right Goldfish can be kept in a bowl, a tank or a pond. They are cold-water fish, and vary in size.

Parrots come from warm countries. They have powerful beaks and are very colourful. They can learn to talk, and are friendly household pets.

Left A hamster should be lifted by placing a hand over the top of the body so that it cannot bite.

42

Some people keep a pony as a pet. A well-trained pony makes a good playmate. Ponies are sure-footed, intelligent and gentle. They eat grass and hay.

Budgerigars are hardy birds and can be kept in an outdoor aviary.

Right Cats make excellent house pets. They are independent animals. They like one meal a day — and a saucer or two of milk.

Below Mice have large eyes and ears and long whiskers. White mice are sometimes kept as pets and can be trained to perform simple tricks.

There are many different breeds of dogs and they can be wonderful friends. Dogs usually sleep in the house. Their coats should be brushed and combed regularly.

The Wonders of Nature

Water shapes the land we live on. The Colorado River in Arizona, in the United States, has worn away a deep, wide gorge through the mountains. This is called the Grand Canyon. The rushing river wears away the rock and many different layers of rock have been bared. The steep sides of the Canyon are like huge steps coloured in red, green, white and brown rocks. Some of the famous gorges in the world have been cut by rivers falling over waterfalls. The Niagara Falls are the most famous waterfalls in the world. They are divided into two falls. The Horseshoe Falls are in Canada and the American Falls are in the United States. The Niagara River plunges over a high cliff into a whirlpool below. Vesuvius, near Naples in Italy, is a famous volcano. A volcano looks like a mountain. It is a hole in the earth's surface. Millions of years ago the earth was very hot. The surface has cooled, but it is still hot inside the earth. When a volcano erupts, molten ash and rock spout out into the air. The mouth of a volcano is called a crater. A spring that throws up hot water from time to time into the air from beneath the surface of the earth is called a geyser. The water often shoots up in great columns. The most

continued on page 46

The Siberian tundra is permanently semi-frozen. Stunted plants grow on the vast marshy plains, which are perpetually covered with snow.

The Blue Grotto, a natural cavern on the north coast of Capri, can only be reached by boat. The entrance is barely 4 feet high.

Wave Rock, Western Australia. This huge rock structure looks like a frozen wave.

Mt Kilimanjaro (19,340 feet), the highest point on the continent of Africa. The name means 'The Great Mountain'.

The Niagara Falls, one of the great natural wonders of the world. The falls produce electric power.

continued from page 44

famous geyser in the world is in Yellowstone National Park. It is called 'Old Faithful'. Ayers Rock in Australia is the largest single block of stone in the world. It varies in colour from mauve to fiery red, depending on the time of day. It is oval-shaped and is built of water-worn pebbles of granite cemented by finer sands. Deserts are lands where few plants grow. Deserts are not always large flat areas of sand. They have rocks and mountains – and oases. An oasis is a fertile place in a desert. There is water at an oasis, and date palms. There are hot deserts and cold deserts. The Sahara is a hot desert. The tundras of Siberia are cold. The tundras stretch for thousands of miles across the north of Russia. The Painted Desert, in Arizona, is beautiful. The sun changes the desert colours from blue, amethyst and yellow to russet, lilac and red. These are only a few of the wonders of nature. There are many others.

Ayers Rock, the largest monolith in the world, is in the northern territory of Australia. It is 2 miles long, 1 mile wide, and rises to a height of 1,100 feet.

Old Faithful in Wyoming (United States), a famous geyser. It erupts every hour, spouting 100 feet of water into the air for about five minutes.

The Painted Desert, a wasteland of brilliantly-coloured pinnacles and valleys, covers a vast area along the Little Colorado River in Arizona.

Mount Fuji, the highest mountain in Japan (12,388 feet). Visitors call it Fujiyama. The Japanese, who consider it a sacred mountain, call it Fuji-San. In the winter it wears a crown of snow. The top of the mountain is often hidden by clouds and its peak contains an extinct volcano crater.

The first white men to discover the Grand Canyon were Spaniards. The canyon rims are covered by thick forests.

The Weather

Everyone talks about the weather. Weather forecasts appear every day in the newspapers and on the television screen. It may be sunny and fine, or dull and rainy. The wind may blow. If there is a storm there will be thunder and lightning. Clouds and winds tell us a lot about the weather. Clouds are made of droplets of water or tiny crystals of ice. The drops fall to earth as rain. When it is very cold ice crystals form instead of droplets of water. They fall to the earth as snow. There is snow and ice all the year round in the Arctic. Some parts of the earth get a great deal of rain, some hardly any. The driest places on earth are the centres of large continents such as the middle of the Sahara and the great Gobi desert of eastern Asia.

There are many different forms of clouds. Light, soft, fluffy clouds are usually a sign of fine weather. Dark, jagged clouds usually mean that it is going to rain or be windy. Weather is made up of the changes that take place from day to day in the air around us. Climate is the kind of weather which a country has year after year. We talk about the climate of a country. But we ask: 'What is the weather like today?' Men who forecast the weather are called meteorologists. They use a thermometer to measure the temperature, a barometer to measure air pressure and a wind gauge to measure the speed of the wind. Balloons and weather satellites carry equipment high into the sky to record and measure weather conditions.

Stratus

Cumulus

Cumulonimbus

Altostratus

Altocumulus

Cirrus

Cirrostratus
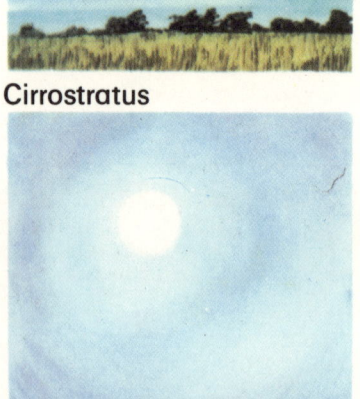

Cirrocumulus

Above The main cloud formations
Right Lightning flashes heat the air and produce thunder.
Below A weather satellite, equipped with television cameras, sends pictures of cloud formations and other information back to earth. It circles the earth several times a day.

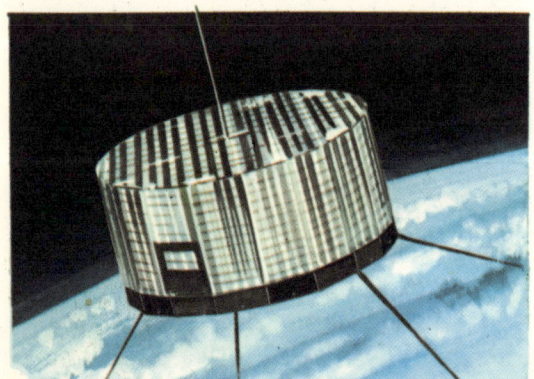

Diagram of the Beaufort Scale

Below Weather ships supply essential reports to the meteorologists or 'met.' men, as they are known. There are several weather ships in the North Atlantic sending in reports from the high seas. Information from many sources is used in forecasts.

Above Snow scene

THE BEAUFORT SCALE

No.	Effects Over Land	m.p.h.
0	Smoke rises vertically	1
1	Smoke drifts	1– 3
2	Leaves rustle	4– 7
3	A light flag flies	8–12
4	Small branches move	13–18
5	Small trees sway	19–24
6	Large branches sway	25–31
7	It is hard to walk against the wind	32–38
8	Twigs break off trees	39–46

A rainbow is an arc of coloured light which appears in showery weather when the sun's light is reflected inside raindrops.

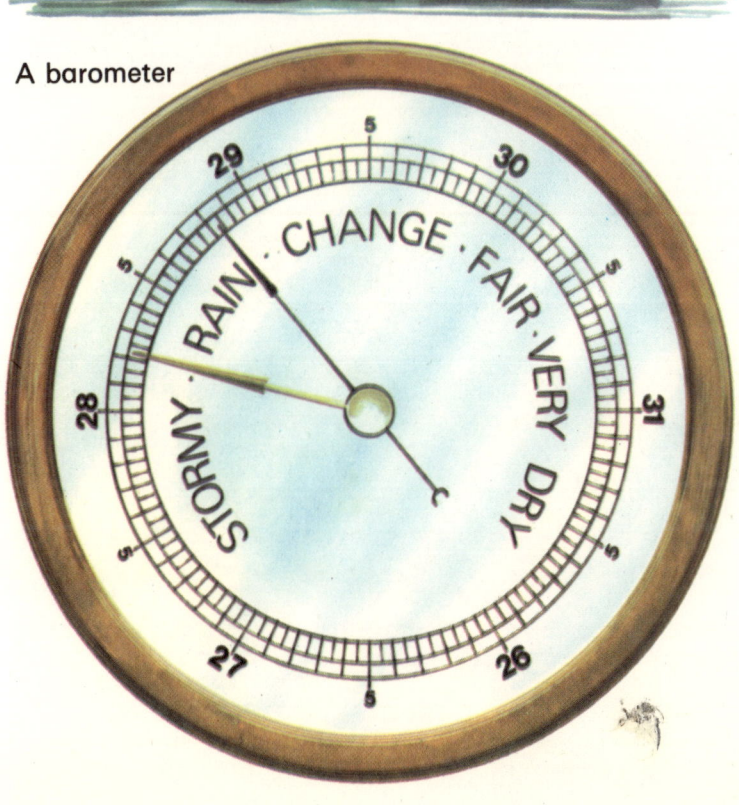

A barometer

Exploring Beneath the Sea

Nearly three-quarters of the surface of the earth is covered by water. The seas and oceans are full of animal and plant life. We need the food and minerals that are in the seas to feed the ever-increasing number of people in the world. We are learning to farm the sea as we do the land. In ancient Greece men dived into the sea and rescued treasure from sunken ships. Divers collected coral and sponges from the bed of the Mediterranean. A man cannot hold his breath for very long. If he wants to stay under water for any length of time he must have a supply of air. Modern divers have equipment which enables them to stay under the water for a long time. Divers can descend quite deep into the ocean. Some divers wear a diving suit with an air tube to the surface. Sometimes divers carry their own air supply in cylinders on their backs. A French diving expert, Jacques Cousteau, invented the aqualung. He also designed the 'Diving Saucer'. This vessel cruised under the water. It carried enough oxygen to last two men twenty-four hours. The bathyscaphe was invented by a Belgian, Auguste Piccard. Men can go down far deeper into the ocean in this than they can in a submarine. Underwater craft like the Diving Saucer, the submarine and the bathyscaphe help men to explore the oceans. We have already found oil, natural gas and coal on the ocean floor. One day much of our water supply will come from the sea.

A submarine is a warship. It can submerge quickly by filling its tanks with seawater. When it surfaces the water is replaced by air.

Professor Piccard designed the 'bathyscaphe' or 'deep ship' to explore the sea bed. The divers ride in an observation chamber suspended from a boat-shaped tank.

Jacques Cousteau's 'Diving Saucer', used for exploring the bed of the ocean. This jet-propelled research vessel can twist and turn, rise and dive under water in the same way as fishes do. Two cameras are mounted outside, as well as a claw which can pick up objects.

A diver moves freely underwater with an aqualung on his back. He wears a light rubber suit, 'frogs' feet' and a diving mask. He hunts with camera, gun or spear.

A diver brings to the surface treasure from the wreck of a ship which may have lain on the bed of the ocean for thousands of years.

Modern nuclear-powered submarines can stay submerged for weeks on end. They have voyaged beneath the pack ice of the North Pole.

Boats and Ships

There are many different kinds of ships. There are cargo ships, and oil tankers, whale catchers and trawlers, yachts, submarines, destroyers, frigates, minesweepers, cruisers and aircraft carriers. There are weather ships, lightships and lifeboats. Passenger liners are like large, comfortable, floating hotels. The first boats were made of logs fastened together. Then man learned to hollow out logs and shape the ends so that they would glide easily through the water. Dugout canoes were used by prehistoric man. The ancient Britons used coracles. Coracles are round boats covered with animal skins. The Eskimos made kayaks from driftwood and sealskins. The Egyptians were the first to build ships. They were rowed by oarsmen.

The early Phoenicians, Greeks, Romans and Vikings used the same type of rowing galley as the Egyptians. The Vikings called their broad, shallow boats 'longships'. They were steered by oars. Then ships were given rudders to steer them by. Larger ships were built. Countries began to trade with one another. Merchant ships carried cargoes of tea, sugar, cotton and manufactured goods. Clipper ships looked like big yachts. Then sail gave way to steam. Big paddle wheels were driven round by a steam engine. The steam turbine took the place of the steam engine. The motor and the diesel engine followed. Now atomic power is being used to propel ships.

Below The Nile was Egypt's natural highway. The earliest Egyptian boats were made from bundles of papyrus (paper reeds) lashed together.

Below The first sea-traders were the Phoenicians. They were brave and adventurous sailors and travelled far in their sturdy, single-masted ships to trade with other countries.

Left The Vikings built fine ships. They rode high out of the water. The Vikings did not depend on oars, they learned the art of sailing.

Below The Pechili trader — the oldest type of Chinese sea-junk. It is flat-bottomed and has a shelter on the deck for the crew.

The *Cutty Sark*, a famous clipper ship, was built like a yacht. She raced half way across the world, carrying valuable cargoes of tea from China to London.

Above The *Victory*, Nelson's flagship at the battle of Trafalgar. She had three decks and 100 guns. *Victory* is now in Portsmouth Harbour, England.

Below The German pocket battleship, the *Admiral Graf Spee.* She was blown to pieces by her own crew in the Battle of the River Plate, the first naval battle of World War II.

Queen Elizabeth 2 – probably the last of the great passenger ships to cross the Atlantic. Jet aircraft are taking a bigger and bigger share of the transatlantic passenger market.

53

Motor Cars

Few modern inventions have had a greater effect on our lives than the motor car. The car was made to take the place of the horse. The first vehicles were driven by steam. The petrol engine was invented by a German called Carl Benz. Another German, named Daimler, designed a car with an internal combustion engine. This was the start of the modern motor car. Early cars looked like the carriages which used to be drawn by horses. At first there were few cars on the roads. In Great Britain, in those early motoring days, no car was allowed on the road unless a man walked in front of it carrying a red flag. The motor industry grew very quickly. In America Henry Ford built a car cheap enough for ordinary people to buy. It was called the Model T Ford. Car-racing began. It is a sport, and a way of testing new designs. A race-track opened in Surrey, England. It was called Brooklands. C. S. Rolls and Henry Royce built large, expensive cars. Then a baby car appeared. It was a four-seater and it was very popular. It was called the Austin Seven. Nowadays the motor car is part of our lives. We are building roads all over the country to make travelling easier. Cars are fitted with heaters, radios, air-conditioners. The driver and passengers can see through large windows. Windscreen-wipers, defrosters and safety-belts are fitted. One day the petrol engine, like the steam engine, will be out of date. Oil engines or diesels are used on many vehicles. A car with a gas turbine engine has already been invented.

Below Daimler's motorised carriage. By the mid-1880s the petrol engine was being used instead of steam to propel road vehicles.

Above The first successful motor vehicle. Built by Richard Trevithick, a Cornishman, it was driven by steam.

The Rolls-Royce 'Silver Ghost', a sporting car which, in 1911, was driven from London to Edinburgh covering 24 miles for each gallon of petrol.

Right Henry Ford, an American, made good cars at popular prices. His Model T Ford was also known as the 'Tin Lizzie'.

Above You can see many small cars like this Italian Fiat on the roads today. Small cars are cheaper to buy and easier to drive and park in crowded cities than larger cars.

Left This is the framework of a car before the body is put on to it.

Brand's Hatch, Britain's Number 1 Grand Prix motor racing circuit, is set in natural surroundings in the hills of north Kent.

Shell

Below Sir Malcolm Campbell's highest speed was reached in 1935 in 'Bluebird'. His speed: 301·13 m.p.h.

Railways

Railways carry passengers and goods. Wagons and carriages are drawn by trains. The first public railway in Britain was called the Surrey Iron Railway. The carriages were pulled by horses. Then George Stephenson built a train driven by steam, called 'Locomotion'. Steam engines burned coal to heat water. The hot water produced steam and the steam pushed the steering rods which made the wheels go round. Before long Great Britain was criss-crossed by a network of railways. Trains travelled faster. They carried food, parcels, mail, newspapers and passengers. They began to run to fixed timetables. Railways were soon built in other countries, too. Railway lines were laid across America from the east coast to the west coast. Trains travelled long distances and special cars were built so that people could eat and sleep during the journey. The United States now has more miles of track than any other country. Underground railways were built. The Trans-Siberian Railway was opened in Russia. The fastest regular railway run in the world is the New Tokaido Express service in Japan. Diesel and electric locomotives have taken the place of steam. Experiments are being made with gas-turbine locomotives. Monorails may soon be carrying passengers above the city streets.

George Stephenson's 'Rocket' which won the first prize of £500 at the Trials on the Rainhill Level of the Liverpool and Manchester Railway in 1829.

The first practicable electric locomotive was built by Werner von Siemens. It hauled visitors round a 900 foot track at the Berlin Trades Exhibition in 1879.

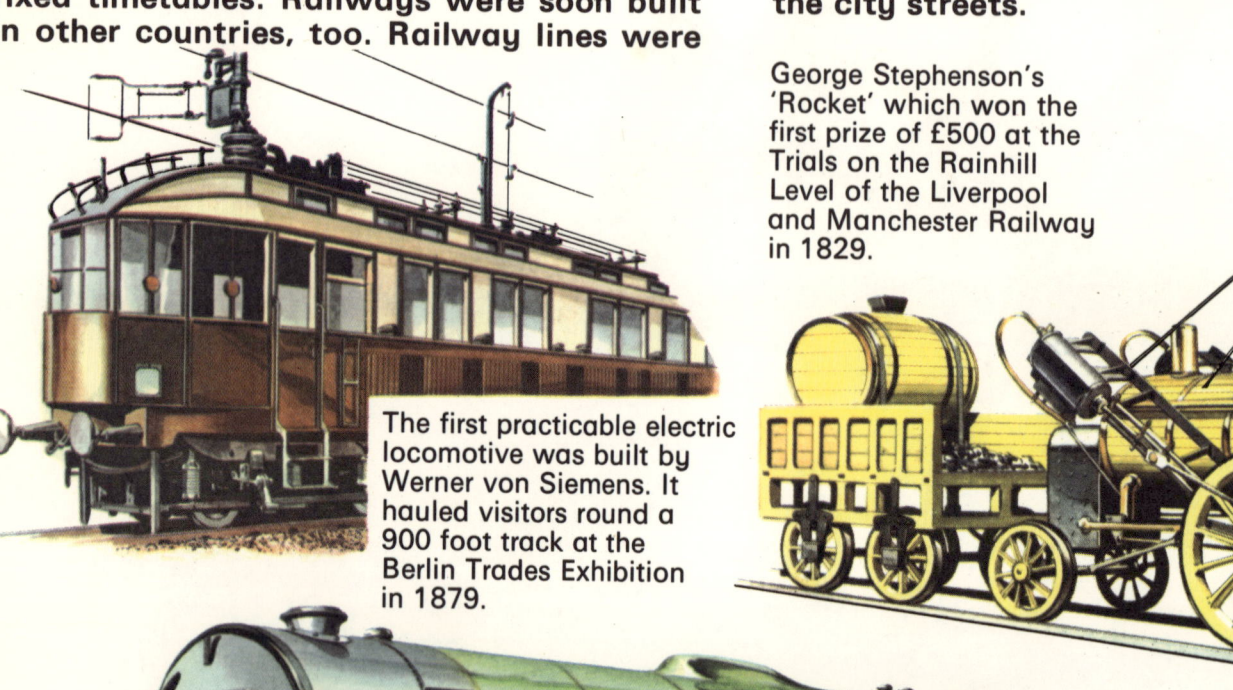

Above Probably the most famous engine in the world, L.N.E.R. Class A 3 Pacific No. 4472 Flying Scotsman.

Right The electrically-powered French *Mistral*, which runs between Paris and Marseilles. Average speed 75 m.p.h.

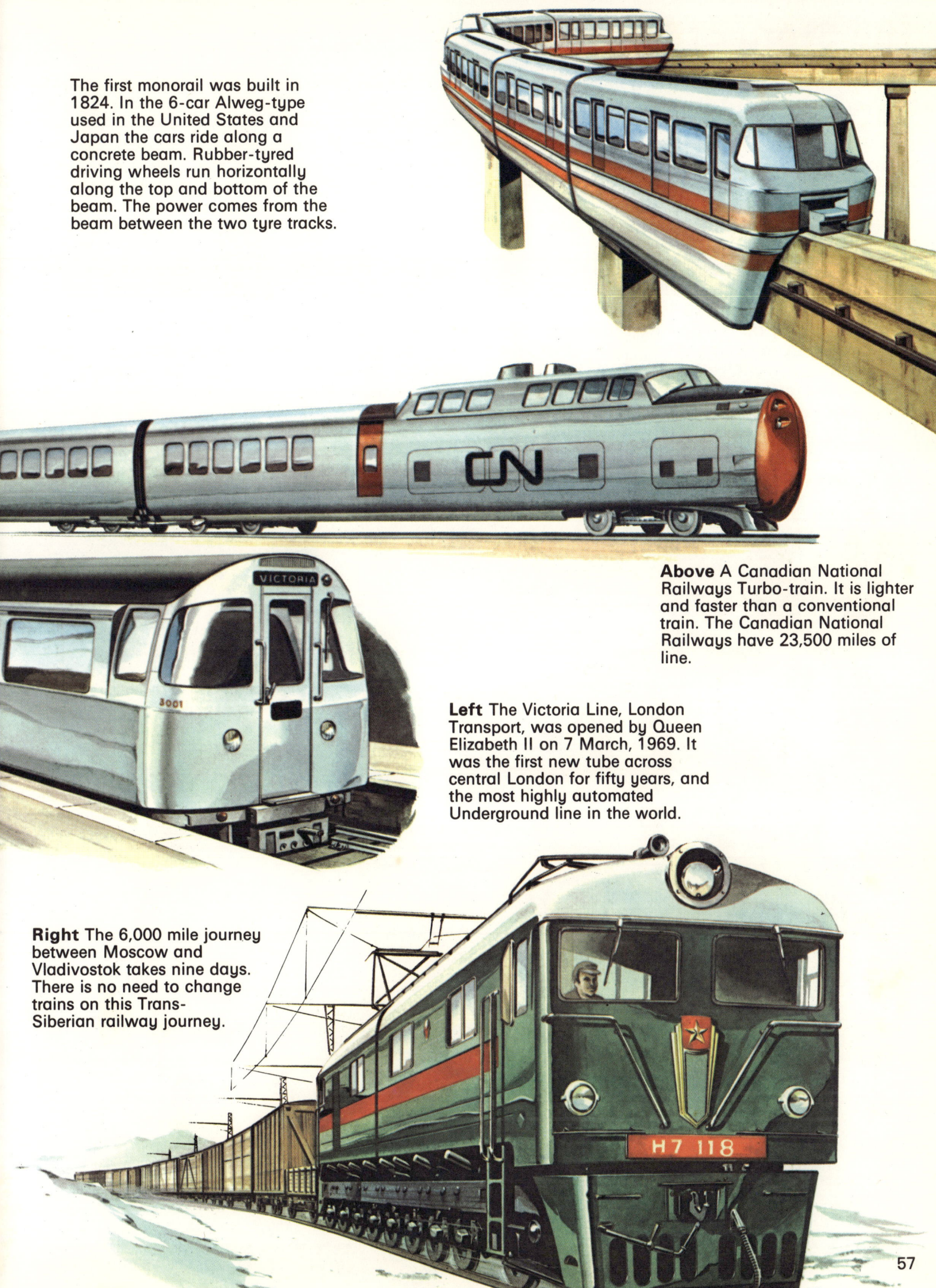

The first monorail was built in 1824. In the 6-car Alweg-type used in the United States and Japan the cars ride along a concrete beam. Rubber-tyred driving wheels run horizontally along the top and bottom of the beam. The power comes from the beam between the two tyre tracks.

Above A Canadian National Railways Turbo-train. It is lighter and faster than a conventional train. The Canadian National Railways have 23,500 miles of line.

Left The Victoria Line, London Transport, was opened by Queen Elizabeth II on 7 March, 1969. It was the first new tube across central London for fifty years, and the most highly automated Underground line in the world.

Right The 6,000 mile journey between Moscow and Vladivostok takes nine days. There is no need to change trains on this Trans-Siberian railway journey.

The Story of Flight

Man has always wanted to fly like the birds. Many people have tried to find out the secret of how birds fly. An Italian, Leonardo da Vinci, drew plans for a flying machine and a parachute. Flying was only a dream in those days. The first flight in the history of man was in a hot air balloon. Two brothers named Montgolfier made a balloon of linen and paper. They decorated it in bright colours. Two passengers climbed aboard. Then a fire was lit underneath the balloon – and it rose up into the air. Man had learned to fly. The first men to fly an aeroplane under its own power were Americans. They were brothers called Wilbur and Orville Wright. They built a tiny aircraft. It had wings, a rudder to steer it by and a propeller. The propeller was driven by an engine of the kind used in motor cars. It stayed up in the air for only a few seconds. Later, a Frenchman, Louis Blériot, flew an aeroplane across the Channel. Then two Englishmen, John Alcock and Arthur Whitten-Brown flew across the Atlantic. There are many different kinds of aircraft. Some aircraft can take off from the deck of a ship. Helicopters do not have wings. They have a propeller on top. This is called a rotor. Modern aeroplanes are propelled by jet engines. Hot gas rushes out of the back of the engine and pushes the plane forward. Jet planes fly high in the sky. They fly at high speeds. Giant airliners carry people to every corner of the world. Now men have landed on the moon. They flew by rocket.

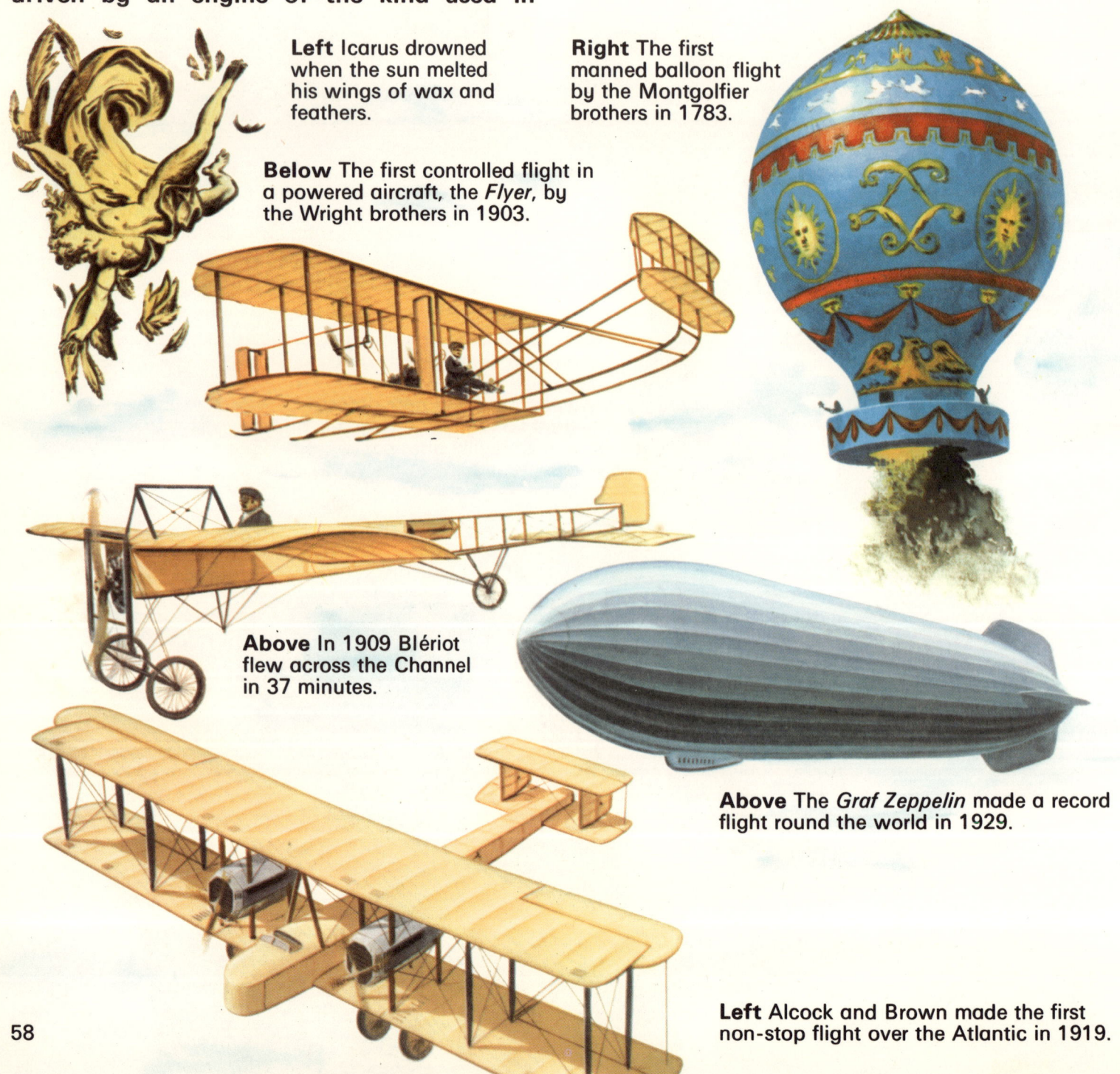

Left Icarus drowned when the sun melted his wings of wax and feathers.

Right The first manned balloon flight by the Montgolfier brothers in 1783.

Below The first controlled flight in a powered aircraft, the *Flyer*, by the Wright brothers in 1903.

Above In 1909 Blériot flew across the Channel in 37 minutes.

Above The *Graf Zeppelin* made a record flight round the world in 1929.

Left Alcock and Brown made the first non-stop flight over the Atlantic in 1919.

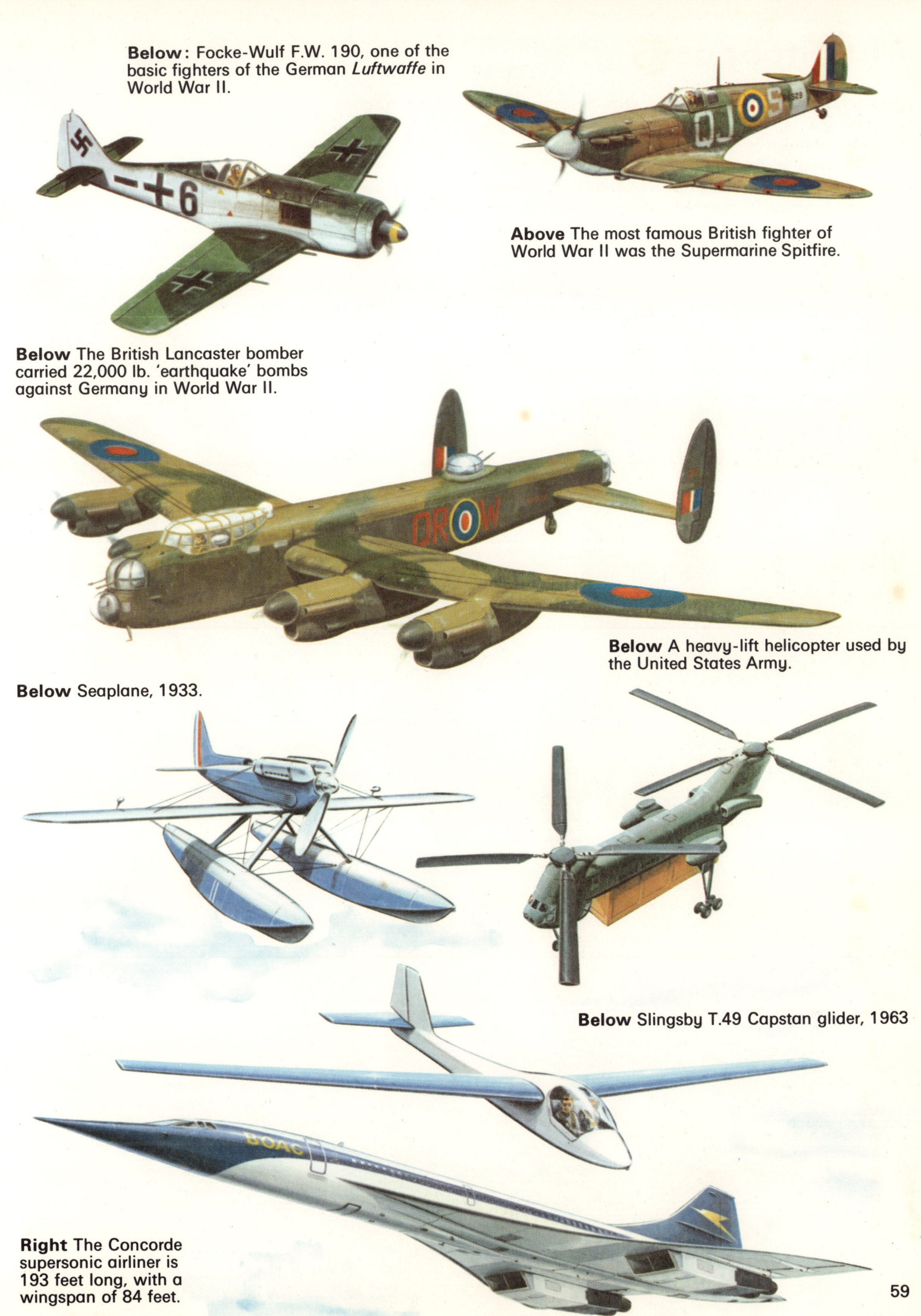

Below: Focke-Wulf F.W. 190, one of the basic fighters of the German *Luftwaffe* in World War II.

Above The most famous British fighter of World War II was the Supermarine Spitfire.

Below The British Lancaster bomber carried 22,000 lb. 'earthquake' bombs against Germany in World War II.

Below A heavy-lift helicopter used by the United States Army.

Below Seaplane, 1933.

Below Slingsby T.49 Capstan glider, 1963

Right The Concorde supersonic airliner is 193 feet long, with a wingspan of 84 feet.

Man in Space

The earth is surrounded by air. Beyond this belt of air there is space. Man can travel through space in craft propelled by rockets. The Russians were the first to send a man-made satellite into space. The first traveller in space was a Russian dog called Laika. Satellites can send useful information back to earth. A satellite carried the first man into space. He was Yuri Gagarin, a Russian. The first men to land on the moon were Americans. Their names were Neil Armstrong and Edwin Aldrin. Their spacecraft was fixed on to the top of a giant rocket. The rocket thrust the spacecraft through the air into

Below left Major Yuri Gagarin, a Russian, was the first man to orbit the earth and return alive. This he did in his spacecraft 'Vostok 1' on 12 April, 1961.

Lift-off for Saturn V, the powerful American rocket which thrust Apollo 11 on its journey to the moon. All American space flights begin from Cape Kennedy, Florida, U.S.A. Space rockets are big. They carry a lot of fuel. The astronauts travel in the capsule. The capsule also contains the instruments, the radio and oxygen. Apollo 11 carried three American astronauts – Neil Armstrong, Edwin Aldrin and Michael Collins – to the moon. It was an historic flight. Man landed on the moon for the first time on 21 July, 1969.

space. We on earth were able to watch on television as the astronauts stepped out of their spacecraft on to the surface of the moon. They collected lunar earth and rocks and brought them back to earth. There is no air in space for astronauts to breathe. They have to take air with them in their spacecraft. When astronauts leave their spacecraft they wear spacesuits. Spacecraft sent to the moon are called probes. We are now sending probes to the planets. Venus and Mars are the planets closest to earth. Soon there may be a space station in orbit. Spacecraft will need something like a garage in space if they are able to go on long journeys and not return to earth for supplies. There would be a workshop, and astronauts would live and sleep in the space station.

Above Neil Armstrong was the first man to set foot on the moon's surface. As he climbed down the ladder from the lunar module he said: 'That's one small step for a man, but one giant leap for mankind.'

Above Spacecraft meet and link up in space. This is called docking.

A space station like this may one day revolve round the earth. Astronauts would be able to live and work in this orbiting hotel. In this way we would find out more about the Universe.

Communications

We use words when we talk. Words are a simple means of communication. There are many other ways in which we can communicate. We can wave our hands, shake hands, nod our heads, smile or frown. Babies cry. Dogs bark and wag their tails. Cats say 'miaow' and purr. Birds sing. Horses neigh. They are all exchanging information. Communication is a very important aspect of our lives. Radio, television, books, pictures, films and music are all means of communication. Deaf people are able to 'talk' by using a sign language. Messages are beaten out on drums. The Incas kept records by tying knots in wools of different lengths, colours and thicknesses. Bells ring out messages of joy, sorrow or warning. Maps and charts are a form of language. Newspapers bring us the news of the world. We can talk to friends on the telephone. Police, fire and ambulance services can bring help quickly when it is needed. We can write a letter – and send it by post. We can send a telegram. Cables carry messages in the form of electric signals. Bundles of wires to carry cables have been laid across the floors of the oceans.

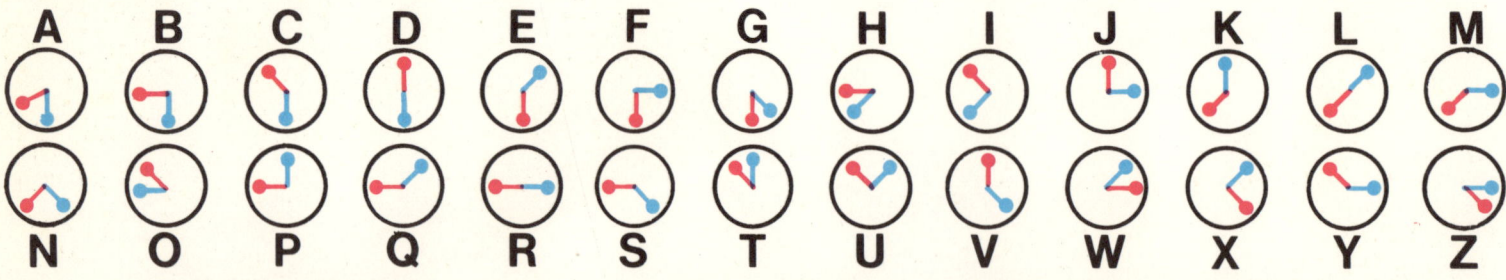

Semaphore, a means of signalling by holding a flag in each hand. The red indicator shows the position of the right arm.

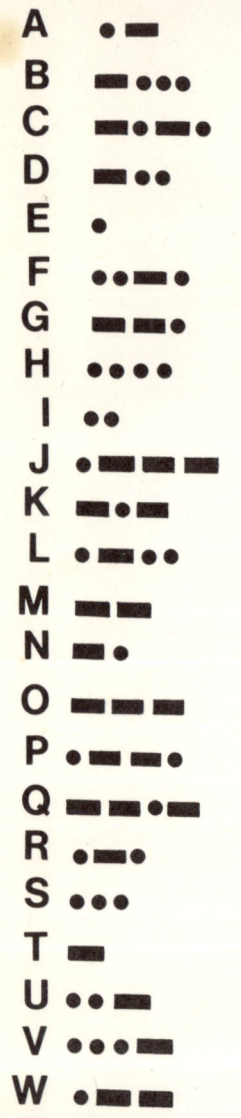

Above A switchroom, International Telephone Exchange.

Right Guglielmo Marconi, an Italian inventor, constructed the first practical radio in 1895.

Left The Morse Code is used to send messages by telegraph. It is a system of dots and dashes based on the alphabet.

Left The Post Office Tower, London. The dish and horn-shaped aerials handle thousands of telephone calls and provide many television channels at the same time.

Left John Logie Baird, a Scotsman, is known as the Father of Television. He made his early experiments using lenses from two cycle lamps, a torch, parts of a radio set, string, sealing wax, glue and an old electric motor. The BBC used the Baird system for seven years, before changing to another.

Above A modern television studio. Note the cameras, their crews, the boom microphones and the big, powerful lights.

Setting up vision input equipment.

Below Communications satellites relay telephone calls and television programmes from one country to another.

Telstar

Early Bird

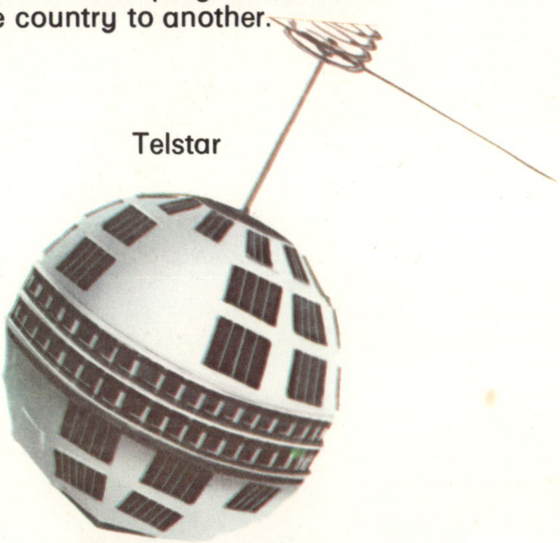

Right Goonhilly Downs earth station. It tracks satellites and through them sends out and receives television, telephone and telegraph signals.

The World of Art

Music, painting, sculpture, writing, pottery, weaving, architecture and dancing are all forms of art. Artists use their personal skill and talent to show us what they see, to record things that happen, to tell us their thoughts, their feelings and the things they dream about. Art gives great pleasure to people in many different ways. Dancing is the oldest of the arts. Melody and rhythm have existed as long as man. Ballet dancers tell a story without using words. Before there were any books wandering minstrels told stories in song. Strolling players acted out comedy and tragedy, drama and panto-mime. The first books were written on long rolls of papyrus, a kind of paper made from reed-like plants. Authors write books. Poets write verse. Composers write music. Actors and actresses take part in plays. Jewellers fashion beautiful brooches, bangles and necklaces of silver and gold. Artists paint on paper with colours mixed with water, or on canvas with colours mixed with oil. Artists who design buildings are called architects. Potters make vases of clay. Long ago man found out that he could take wet clay and shape it with his hands into bowls and jars. Sculptors work with clay, wood, metal and stone. They use tools to fashion the materials into statues and lovely shapes. Weavers make pictures called tapestries.

Vincent van Gogh, a Dutch painter of the Expressionist school. Here he is painting sunflowers.

Below Le Corbusier, a Swiss architect, rebuilt the bombed church of Notre-Dame at Ronchamp, in 1952, in a completely new style. He designed houses as 'machines for living'.

Leonard Bernstein, an American composer, conductor and pianist. A conductor leads a musical group, using a baton and hand motions to tell the musicians how to play the piece.

The great English ballerina Margot Fonteyn and her partner Rudolf Nureyev.

Sir Jacob Epstein, sculptor. He carved and modelled large figures and portraits in bronze.

Left Pottery is the general name given to all kinds of ware made from clay and other minerals when they have been 'fired' — that is, hardened by heat in the potter's kiln. Pottery is no longer made entirely by hand.

Plays are performed in a theatre. This open-air theatre with the seating in tiers, is in Turkey, at Priene.

Right The weaver weaves a tapestry on a frame or 'loom'. Simple weaving is done by interlacing threads over and under each other.

Musical Instruments

There are three groups of musical instruments — stringed instruments, wind instruments and percussion. Stringed instruments are played by drawing a bow across the strings or by plucking the strings with the fingertips. The violin, viola, cello and double bass are stringed instruments. The strings of a harp are plucked by the fingers. The strings of a piano are hit by hammers. The player pushes down keys. This makes little hammers strike the strings. The dulcimer, the psaltery, the hurdy-gurdy and the zither are all stringed instruments. Wind instruments are played by blowing air into a hollow tube. Woodwind instruments have reeds inside them. Brass instruments do not. The flute, oboe, clarinet, saxophone, recorder, piccolo and bassoon belong to the woodwind family. The horn, trumpet, cornet, trombone and tuba belong to the brass family. Not all woodwind instruments are made of wood — some are made of metal or ivory. Brass instruments are not all made of brass — some are made of silver, copper, horn, ivory or wood. Drums, triangles, cymbals, glockenspiel and xylophones are percussion instruments. They are struck to produce sound. Triangles are hit with a steel 'beater'. Cymbals are clashed together. Tambourines are shaken. Drums are made of skin stretched over a frame. Drum-sticks are used to beat the drum. An orchestra is made up of many musicians playing together on different instruments, directed by a conductor. If there are no stringed instruments the group of musicians is called a band.

Below The trumpet has a narrow, long bore with a cup-shaped mouthpiece at one end and an opening, or bell, at the other.

Left This violin was made by Antonio Stradivari, one of the greatest violinmakers of all time. He was born at Cremona, Italy.

Right A bass clarinet. The clarinet is the leading instrument in military bands. It is sometimes used as a solo instrument.

Above Africans are good at making musical instruments. This drum comes from West Africa.

Left The harpsichord is a keyboard instrument. This illustration shows one made by Jan Ruckers in Antwerp in 1634. It is now at Ham House, Richmond, England.

ACTA VIRVM PROBANT · 1634

Right The percussion section of an orchestra includes the timpani, the snare drum, the bass drum, cymbals, gongs, bells, triangle and tambourine.

Above Some stringed instruments, such as the guitar, are played by plucking the strings to produce notes. This can be done with the fingers or with a small piece of wood known as a plectrum.

Above Long hours of practice are needed to become a good pianist. Grand pianos are large and expensive. Smaller pianos are more practical for the home.

Sports

People of all ages enjoy taking part in sports. Sports are fun. For adults sports are a relaxation from their daily work. Some people like sports which give them a lot of exercise. Others prefer sports which make them think. Some games can be played by one person. These include golf, bowling, archery and swimming. Swimming exercises every muscle of the body. Tennis, boxing, fencing and wrestling need an opponent. Tennis is played by one player each side (singles), or two players each side (doubles). Team sports need fast action – and team work. Team work teaches people how to work with others towards a common goal. People all over the world enjoy playing games such as football, cricket, baseball, basket-ball, hockey and ice-hockey. All sports are competitive – and exciting. Sports in which a person, or a team, competes against another person or team are called athletics. The Olympic Games were one of the first sports festivals. They were held, originally, in Greece. The modern Games are great international meetings of athletics, held in different countries. Competitors from many countries take part in the sports. The Track events include all the running races – except the cross-country race. The Field events include the long jump, high jump, pole vault, throwing the discus, throwing the hammer, and putting the weight. King Henry VIII of England was a keen hammer-thrower. Sports teach sportsmanship. A good sport is a person who can win without boasting, and who can accept defeat with good grace.

Young and old enjoy sports. Many friendships are made playing games.

Cricket

Diving

Football

Eventing

Individual sports are popular. Team sports provide lessons in teamwork. Sportsmanship is an important part of life.

Tennis

Boxing

Hurdling